FROM EARTH TO THE STARS

THE BENEFITS OF SPACEFLIGHT AND SPACE EXPLORATION

JASON PORTERFIELD

Britannica
Educational Publishing

IN ASSOCIATION WITH

ROSEN
EDUCATIONAL SERVICES

Published in 2018 by Britannica Educational Publishing (a trademark of Encyclopædia Britannica, Inc.) in association with The Rosen Publishing Group, Inc., 29 East 21st Street, New York, NY 10010

Distributed exclusively by Rosen Publishing. To see additional Britannica Educational Publishing titles, go to rosenpublishing.com.

First Edition

Britannica Educational Publishing
J.E. Luebering: Executive Director, Core Editorial
Andrea R. Field: Managing Editor, Compton's by Britannica

Rosen Publishing
Kathy Kuhtz Campbell: Senior Editor
Nelson Sá: Art Director
Brian Garvey: Series Designer
Greg Tucker: Book Layout
Cindy Reiman: Photography Manager
Karen Huang: Photo Researcher

Library of Congress Cataloging-in-Publication Data
Names: Porterfield, Jason, author.
Title: The benefits of spaceflight and space exploration / Jason Porterfield.
Description: First edition. | New York, NY : Britannica Educational Publishing in association with Rosen Educational Services, 2018. | Series: From Earth to the stars | Audience: Grades 5 to 8. | Includes bibliographical references and index.
Identifiers: LCCN 2016057939| ISBN 9781680486636 (library bound : alk. paper) | ISBN 9781680486612 (pbk. : alk. paper) | ISBN 9781680486629 (6-pack : alk. paper)
Subjects: LCSH: Space flight--Juvenile literature. | Aerospace engineering--Juvenile literature. | Technological innovations--Juvenile literature. | Outer space--Exploration--Juvenile literature.
Classification: LCC TL793 .P577 2018 | DDC 629.4--dc23
LC record available at https://lccn.loc.gov/2016057939

Manufactured in the United States of America

Photo credits: Cover, p. 1 NASA/Bridget Caswell; cover and back cover (background) nienora/Shutterstock.com; pp. 5, 7, 9, 15, 23, 35 NASA; p. 10 Sean Pavone/Shutterstock.com; p. 12 Adapted from information from Encyclopaedia Britannica, Inc. (source: NASA Goddard Space Flight Center); p. 13 National Severe Storms Laboratory/NOA; p. 14 NOAA; p. 17 Courtesy of the U.S. Geological Survey; p. 19 Anatoly Tiplyashin/Shutterstock.com; p. 21 Blausen Medical Communications Inc., CC BY 3.0; p. 25 Vstock LLC/VStock/Thinkstock; p. 26 NASA/JHUAPL/SWRI; p. 27 NASA/JPL-Caltech/MSSS; p. 29 NASA, ESA, and K. Noll (STScl); p. 32 NASA/JPL/Space Science Institute; p. 36 Walter Jaffe/Leiden Observatory, Holland Ford/ JHU/STScI, and NASA; p. 37 Sidharth Nikam/NASA; p. 39 NASA/Ames/JPL-Caltech; interior pages graphic pp. 7, 13, 19, 26, 34 Hallowedland/Shutterstock.com.

On the cover: NASA engineers test a flywheel motor built for a heart pump that was designed to help children born with only one heart ventricle.

CONTENTS

INTRODUCTION

Spaceflight has taken humans to the moon and propelled a probe past the limits of the solar system. It has enabled people to maintain space stations and place thousands of artificial (man-made) satellites in Earth's orbit. But what do human beings gain by venturing into space? Considering all the opportunities and mysteries to be investigated on Earth—not to mention problems to be solved—what's the point of dedicating resources to spaceflight?

To begin with, space exploration satisfies a basic curiosity about worlds beyond our own. It's human nature to want to explore the unknown. Spaceflight has yielded discoveries and wonders that have inspired writers and artists and that have answered some religious and philosophical questions while raising new ones. On a more practical level, space exploration has helped to foster enthusiasm for science in general. Landmark space missions have captured the public imagination, and educational programs related to space exploration have engaged students in science.

Along with its ability to inspire, space exploration has more tangible, or concrete, benefits. Of course it has greatly advanced scientific knowledge of Earth and the rest of the universe. Beyond that, however, space exploration has also provided technologies and products that most people take for granted. Today's advances in space exploration may yield tomorrow's benefits, from space tourism to the diversion of asteroids that would otherwise collide with Earth.

Crew members aboard the ISS celebrate Christmas in 2016. More than two hundred people from eighteen different countries have visited the ISS, which has been occupied continuously since 2000.

Spaceflight fosters international cooperation among government agencies, scientific bodies, industries, and organizations. Some large-scale projects, such as the International Space Station (ISS), would not have been possible without collaboration. Space exploration and research serves as an arena in which countries work together peacefully toward shared goals, even when they may be at odds concerning other issues. The "space race" between the Soviet Union and the United States during the twentieth century contributed to many milestones in space exploration. Today, the United States and Russia cooperate on many missions, especially those involving the ISS. The Outer Space Treaty of 1967 established that nations cannot claim outer space as sovereign territory and forbade installing weapons in space.

Spaceflight isn't a sure thing. Successful missions will be countered by occasional failures and even tragedies. But the unexpected setbacks will be matched by unexpected benefits. As long as human beings set their eyes and ambitions toward space, the resulting discoveries and breakthroughs will make the effort worthwhile.

CHAPTER 1

KEEPING THE WORLD CONNECTED

The space age began on October 4, 1957, when the Soviet Union launched the first artificial satellite to orbit Earth. *Sputnik 1* weighed 184 pounds (84 kilograms). Its maximum distance from Earth was 584 miles (940 kilometers). It circled Earth every ninety-six minutes and remained in orbit until early 1958, when it fell back and burned in Earth's atmosphere.

Today, nearly 1,500 operational artificial satellites orbit Earth. Many more satellites, now dead, are classified

As this model of *Sputnik 1* shows, the first artificial satellite was about the size of a basketball. It was launched into Earth orbit by the Soviet Union in 1957.

as space debris. More than five hundred of the operational satellites were launched by the United States. Most satellites orbit Earth in low Earth orbit (LEO)—between one hundred and one thousand miles (160 km and 1,600 km) above Earth—or geostationary orbit (GEO)—22,236 miles (35,786 km) above Earth.

PHONING HOME AND TUNING IN

The major application of artificial satellites in the modern world is to provide long-distance communication links. In addition to launching the space age, *Sputnik 1* ushered in a new era in communications technology. For its first twenty-two days in orbit, before its battery ran down, the satellite transmitted signals back to Earth. In 1962, the United States launched Telstar 1, the first satellite capable of two-way communication. It transmitted live television images between the United States and Europe, as well as the first phone call transmitted by satellite.

A satellite consists of three main components. The communications system receives a signal from Earth, amplifies the signal, and retransmits it back to Earth, where it can be received over a wide geographic area. The propulsion system includes the rockets that propel the satellite and is capable of adjusting the satellite's position in space. Finally, solar panels provide power to the satellite. A communications satellite can function for up to twenty years.

Many communications satellites operate in GEO, meaning that they are fixed over one specific location

Telstar 1 was launched by NASA on July 10, 1962. Two days later it transmitted the first live television signals across the Atlantic Ocean, between the United States and Europe.

above Earth's surface. These satellites provide a signal to a vast geographical area. Three GEO satellites can provide global coverage. But a signal from a GEO satellite is very slightly delayed. Therefore, mobile and voice services usually utilize satellites in lower orbits.

Today, communication satellites provide various services to broadcasters, internet service providers (ISPs), governments, the military, and other sectors. These include three types of communication services: telecommunications, broadcasting, and data communications. Telecommunication services include telephone calls and services provided to telephone companies, as well as wireless, mobile, and cellular network providers. Broadcasting services include radio and television delivered directly to households as well as programming received by cell phones and other mobile devices. Data communications involve the transfer of data. A significant amount of internet traffic goes through satellites, making ISPs one of the largest customers for satellite services.

WATCHING AND NAVIGATING THE GLOBE

Satellites in space can gather a wealth of information about activities on the ground. Optical satellites transmit aerial images of Earth's surface. Navigational satellites identify the positions of objects on Earth, allowing for highly precise navigation.

Military spy satellites are used for surveillance and reconnaissance—monitoring activities of other nations. One of the earliest US satellite programs, the Discoverer series launched in 1959, consisted of experimental reconnaissance satellites. In addition to collecting images, spy satellites can include instruments such as radar, receivers to intercept radio transmissions, and sensors capable of detecting nuclear radiation.

Satellite dishes receive digital signals directly from communication satellites. Satellite TV has a much larger range than broadcast TV, which transmits and receives signals using ground-based antennas.

INTELSAT

The development of satellite technology in the late 1950s and early 1960s paved the way for a global communications satellite industry. In 1964, the telecommunications agencies of eighteen countries, including the United States, founded the International Telecommunications Satellite Consortium (Intelsat) to develop technologies for satellite communications. Intelsat launched its first satellite, Early Bird (also called Intelsat 1), in 1965. Four years later, the global network of Intelsat satellites broadcast the landing of the first human on the moon live to more than six hundred million television viewers. In the years that followed, many events that were watched worldwide, like the Olympic Games or the World Cup, used the Intelsat system. After becoming a private company in 2001, Intelsat continued to provide global communication services through a network of some fifty satellites.

Navigational satellites transmit data about location directly to a receiver in a piece of equipment such as a Global Positioning System (GPS) device or a cell phone. Most navigational satellites are located in medium Earth orbit (MEO), about 12,500 miles (20,000 km) above Earth. It takes at least two dozen satellites to provide continuous worldwide coverage for users. A receiver on Earth calculates a position based on signals transmitted by four different satellites overhead.

The general term for a system that provides global coverage is a Global Navigation Satellite System (GNSS). Americans are most familiar with GPS, which was developed by the Department of Defense for military use beginning in

The Navstar GPS system consists of a network of satellites that orbit Earth and transmit navigation data to users on the ground.

1973. Today, the Navstar GPS system consists of thirty-one satellites orbiting Earth. It is used across the world as a navigation aid for ships, commercial jets, automobiles, train locomotives, tractors, and even people on foot. Other GNSS systems in use or under development include Russia's GLONASS, Europe's Galileo, and China's Compass (sometimes referred to as BeiDou-2).

Satellite transmissions, including both images and positioning data, can be valuable in surveying and mapping Earth's surface. Surveyors and mapmakers use GPS systems to facilitate data collection in places that might be isolated or difficult to reach in person.

CHAPTER 2

UNDERSTANDING EARTH

Satellites are generally categorized as either scientific or applied, depending on their function. Scientific satellites carry instruments for collecting information on physical phenomena in space. Applied satellites gather information on Earth's atmosphere, image the planet's surface, and identify geological phenomena. These data are put to a variety of practical applications, from forecasting the weather to assisting farmers in choosing crops to guiding response to natural disasters. Satellite data also help advance scientific understanding of Earth sciences such as geology, meteorology, and oceanography.

Meteorologists at the National Oceanic and Atmospheric Administration (NOAA) study weather maps generated from satellite data.

METEOROLOGY

Meteorological satellites (weather satellites) use highly sensitive instruments to obtain data for use in the computer-generated atmosphere models that are the basis of modern weather forecasting. Satellite meteorology came into being with the launching of the first weather satellite in 1960. Weather satellites now monitor the global atmosphere, adding immense amounts of information to the meteorologist's daily database. Many meteorological satellites are positioned in GEO orbit. They provide continuous images of cloud patterns over large areas of Earth's surface. Other

A satellite image released by NOAA shows Hurricane Katrina—one of the most destructive hurricanes in US history—approaching the Gulf of Mexico coast in 2005.

CLIMATE CHANGE

Satellites are an invaluable tool in observing the consequences of human activity on Earth's surface. In particular, weather and climate satellites gather data that help scientists understand climate change. Satellites can track factors such as rates of deforestation and measures of certain gases in the atmosphere that contribute to climate change. They can also monitor the impact of climate change, such as shrinking ice caps, rising sea levels, and decreased annual snow cover. Such information has become increasingly valuable as concern over the long-term effects of climate change has grown.

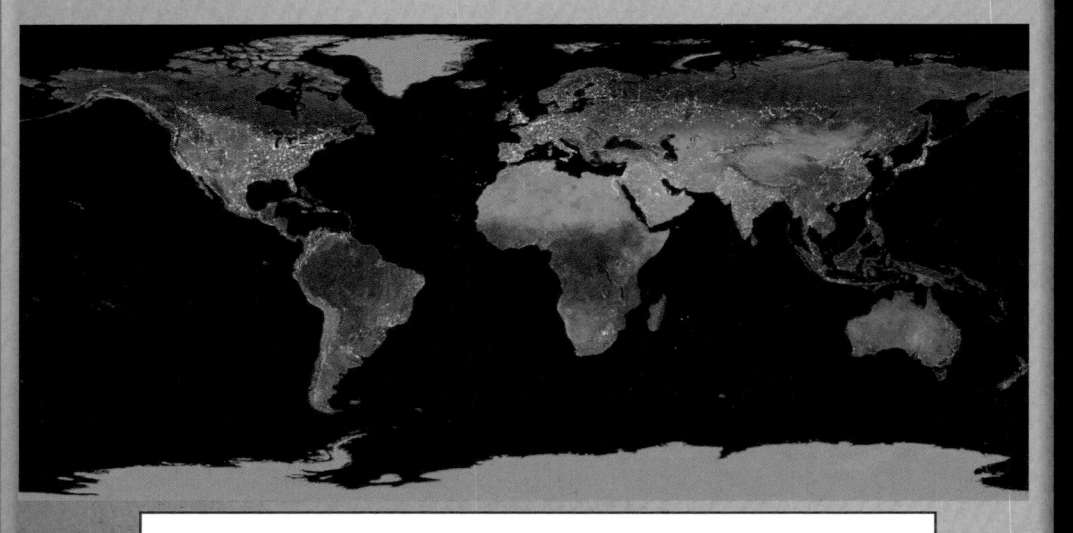

Satellite observation of Earth's surface and atmosphere helps scientists understand climate change. One potential consequence of climate change is rising sea levels, which would cause coastal flooding (areas in red) worldwide.

weather satellites circle Earth at lower altitudes near the north and south poles. Because polar-orbiting satellites fly closer to Earth's surface, they are able to obtain more detailed data about changing atmospheric conditions.

Weather satellites are capable of making global observations, gathering data on areas such as the oceans, which are difficult to monitor through other means. They capture images that make it possible to detect and track weather systems from the moment they begin to form. Remote sensors mounted on the satellite also send back streams of data on atmospheric conditions.

Virtually every segment of society benefits from weather forecasts: the aviation, maritime, and energy industries; potable-water-management and pollution-control agencies; agricultural organizations; defense departments; and, of course, the general public. In particular, weather satellites provide critical data in tracking the stages of hurricane development and improving predictions in times of other disasters such as floods and droughts. Given the importance of accurate weather forecasts, most governments, many universities, and some private corporations sponsor meteorological research programs that range from investigations of the atmosphere to improved methods for modifying the weather.

TRACKING CHANGES

Satellites are used to collect data about Earth's atmosphere and surface, including its land, bodies of water, and ice

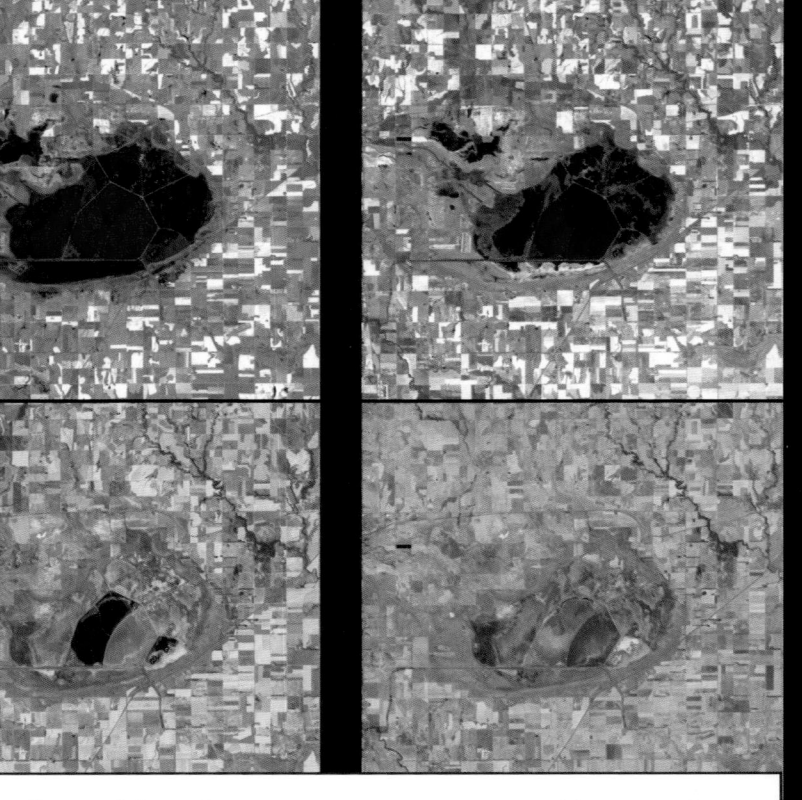

The effects of drought are apparent in a series of four Landsat images of the Cheyenne Bottoms Wildlife Wetlands area in Kansas taken between 2010 and 2012. In just over two years, the marsh virtually disappeared through evaporation.

cover. Satellites measure the composition of the atmosphere, map the tides, determine wind speed and direction, track the motion of Earth's crust, measure Earth's gravity field, and much more. Data provided by satellites can help people monitor disasters such as earthquakes, volcanoes, and fires.

One of the longest running Earth observation satellite programs is Landsat. The first Landsat satellites, launched in the 1970s, were primarily designed to collect information about Earth's natural resources, including the location of mineral deposits and the condition of forests and farming regions. Today, Landsat continues to monitor land conditions around the world. By comparing images taken by Landsat satellites from year to year, scientists have been able to measure changes in land use, such as the conversion of forests to pastureland.

The data collected by satellites have many practical applications. Satellite monitoring helps farmers manage crops and track drought conditions. It can help predict the spread of diseases that affect humans as well as diseases or pests that affect crops. It can provide information in time of disaster, such as the extent of floods or the impact of volcanic activity, that cannot be obtained on the ground. Satellites enable scientists to monitor ecosystems—living organisms interacting with their physical environment. They can help identify energy and mineral resources, improve forest management, and monitor the growth of cities worldwide.

CHAPTER 3

THE TECHNOLOGY OF SPACE

Research and development for spaceflight programs has led to innovations that benefit the daily lives of ordinary people. In many cases, technological advances developed for spaceflight have been found to serve useful purposes completely unrelated to their original function. These by-products of space research are known as "spin-offs." In the United States, the National Aeronautics and

NASA engineers had to design small cameras for interplanetary missions. This work led to the invention of a type of pixel sensor that is now used in most devices that capture digital images, such as digital cameras and smartphones.

Space Administration (NASA) has made possible thousands of spin-off products and services. In some cases, a spin-off is commercialized by a private company that is granted access to NASA technology or expertise, sometimes by being licensed to develop a patent held by NASA. In others, the product or service is developed by a partnership between NASA and a private company from the start.

BETTER MEDICINE THROUGH SPACEFLIGHT

One of the most critical aspects of manned spaceflight missions is keeping astronauts safe and healthy. An astronaut in space who requires medical care does not have access to medical specialists or hospital equipment. In addition, some conditions of spaceflight, such as the acceleration of the launch vehicle and weightlessness in orbit, can have significant physical consequences on the body. Researchers are constantly working on developing new medical instruments and procedures that can be used in space. Many of these have proved valuable on Earth as well.

Some medical advancements have resulted from technology transfer from research and development related to space missions. For example, a device developed for the Hubble Space Telescope has been adapted for use in noninvasive screening for breast cancer. Foam insulation used on the space shuttle has proved to be an effective material for making molds for artificial limbs. Robotic devices similar to those developed to complete repair work on the International

Space Station can be used to perform minimally invasive surgery. Spaceflight technology was crucial in the development of medical imaging and ultrasound techniques. Other medical devices that had their origins in the space program include implantable defibrillators and insulin pumps and a device that improves the efficiency of cardiopulmonary resuscitation (CPR) for cardiac arrest patients.

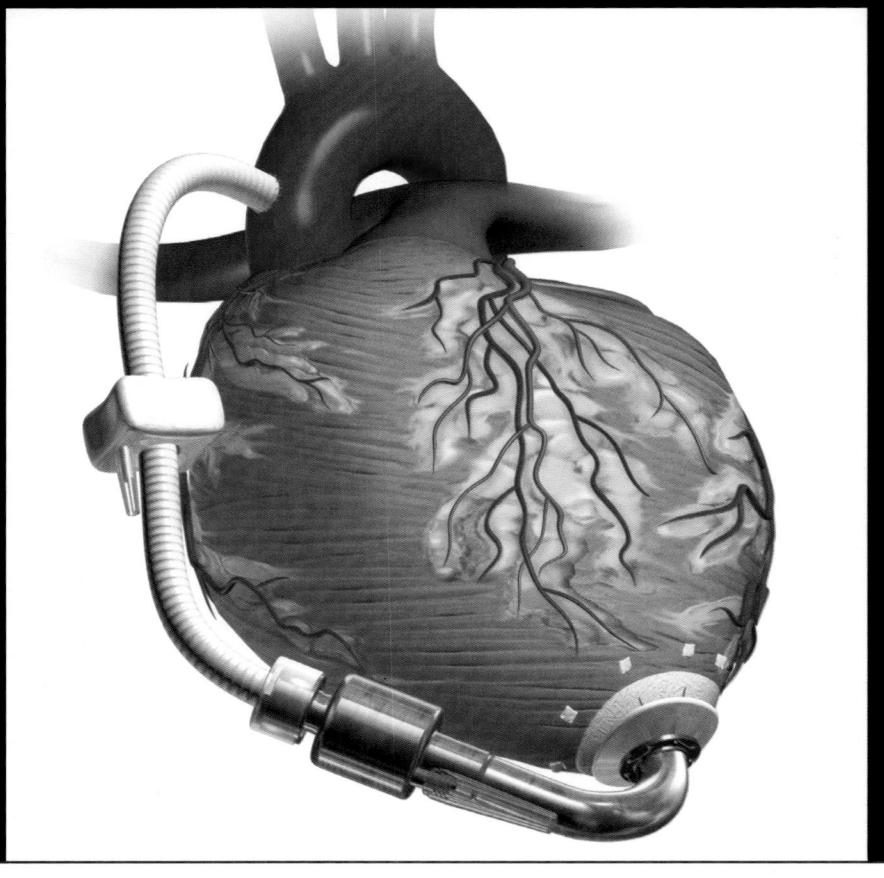

NASA researchers familiar with the flow of fuel through rocket engines helped design a cardiac pump that keeps blood circulating in patients awaiting a heart transplant.

Some of the equipment developed for use in space has been transferred down to Earth. Controls were developed that allow astronauts to use eye movements or voice commands to operate devices. This technology is now used to give people who have a disability more control over their surroundings. The cooling system in space suits can be used in a medical setting as a treatment for various conditions.

ADVANCES FOR INDUSTRY AND CONSUMERS

Spin-offs of space research have benefited a number of industries and can be found in many products that people take for

FARMING IN SPACE

The ISS, situated in low Earth orbit, is a permanently manned research and observation outpost. Assembly began in 1998 and the station became fully operational in 2009, although modifications and improvements continue. Astronauts from eighteen countries have visited the ISS.

Facilities on the ISS allow scientists to conduct experiments and make observations related to biology, Earth sciences, physical sciences, and human health. The ISS also serves as a testing facility in planning and preparing for future space exploration, such as a manned mission to Mars. An exciting area of research has been space-farming technology, which could be vital for sustaining astronauts on long-term spaceflights. In 2015, astronauts ate space-grown produce—romaine lettuce—for the first time.

granted in their everyday lives. Technologies used on spacecraft have been transferred directly to other modes of transportation. For example, anti-icing techniques used on aircraft and train tracks were developed using NASA technology. Public safety has also benefited from applications spun off from space technology. Heat- and flame-resistant materials used in space suits have been incorporated into gear for firefighting, for example, and a water-filtration system designed for the ISS can be used to provide affordable, clean drinking water on Earth. An aluminized plastic blanket developed for the space program, small enough to be folded up and carried in a pocket, is useful for rescue work and in other settings.

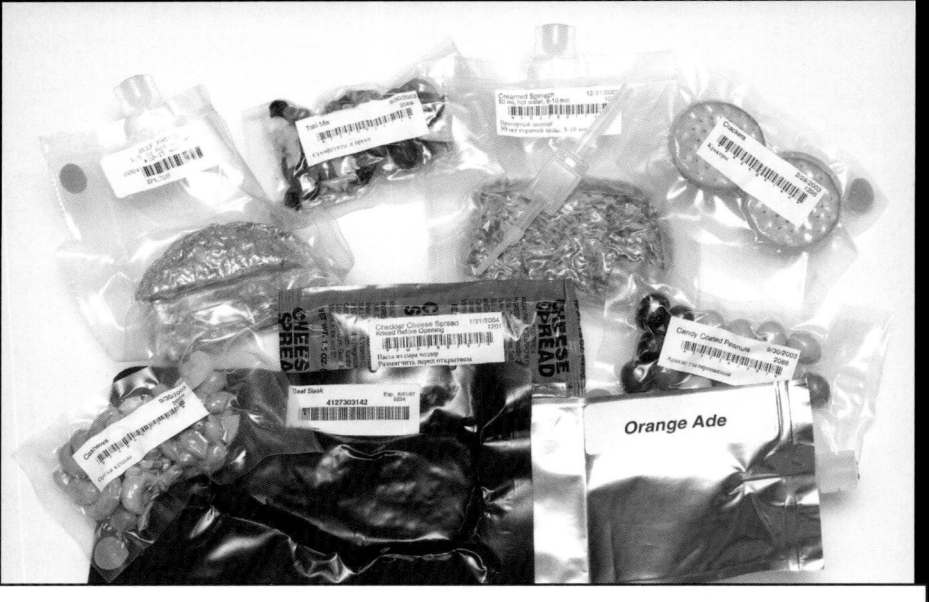

When NASA consulted Pillsbury for help in preparing safe, prepackaged food for astronauts during spaceflight, the company developed a rigorous system to prevent contamination in food production. This system became standard in the food industry.

Some food-safety standards also originated with the space program—NASA worked with the food company Pillsbury to develop a system that would ensure the quality of pre-packaged food for astronauts.

New materials, processes, and products developed through space research have also benefited construction and manufacturing. These innovations include improved structural designs, a powdered lubricant, conductive fibers, and novel fiberglass materials. Shock absorbers designed to withstand a shuttle launch have been incorporated into buildings and bridges constructed in earthquake zones. Advances in computing developed for spaceflight missions have also been spun off. These include hardware improvements, such as innovative circuit boards, specialized software, and virtual reality products. Research into solar cells, which power many satellites and other unmanned spacecraft, has resulted in advances that have improved solar panel technology on Earth.

Consumers benefit from spaceflight programs spin-offs ranging from clothing to baby food. Some shoes incorporate soles based on space suit engineering. Memory foam had its origins in the NASA space program. Research into nutrition led to the discovery of a nutrient that is now used to enrich baby formulas. The Dustbuster handheld vacuum cleaner and other advances in cordless tools were the result of a NASA partnership with Black & Decker. A minuscule tuning fork developed to serve as a timing device in spacecraft is now used in highly accurate wristwatches.

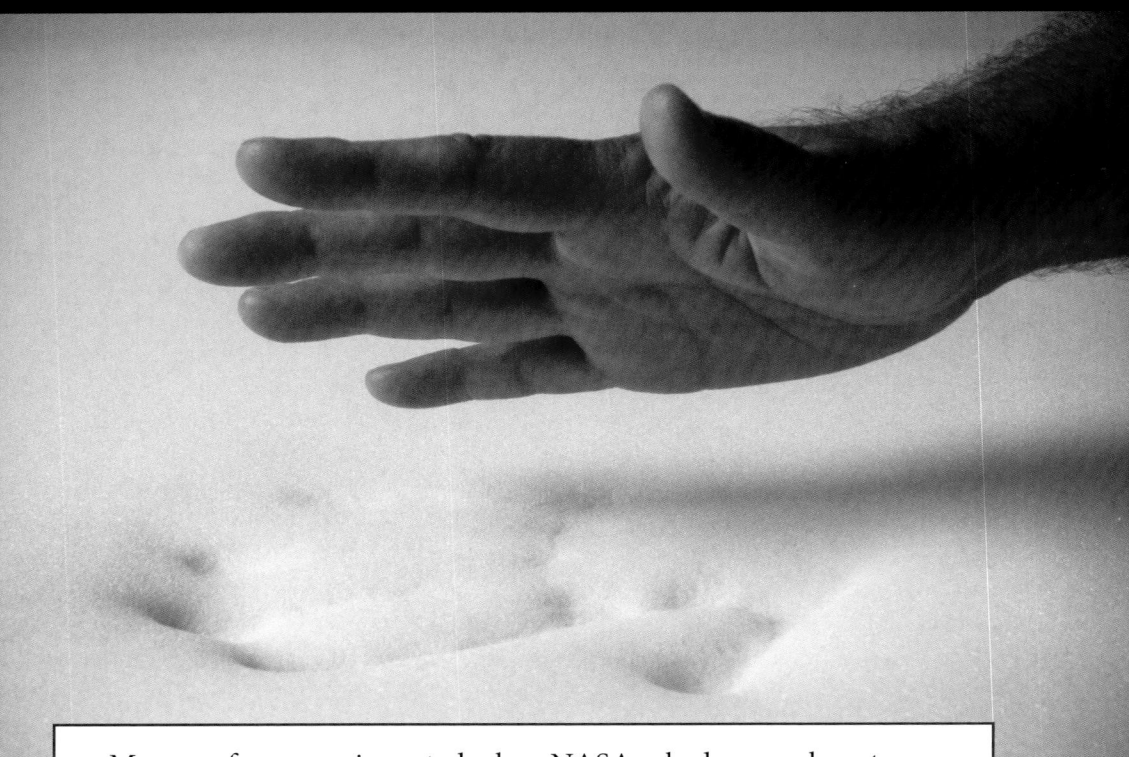

Memory foam was invented when NASA asked researchers to develop airplane seats that would better protect test pilots in the event of a crash. The material is now widely used in mattresses, pillows, couches, shoes, and many other products.

NASA technology led to improvements in two different types of orthodontic braces for teeth. An arch wire made of an alloy called nitinol is used in some braces. Originally designed to extend solar panels outward from satellites in space, nitinol returns to its original shape when activated by heat, whether the source is the sun or body temperature in the mouth. Another material, a translucent ceramic, is used for newer "invisible" braces.

CHAPTER 4

GETTING TO KNOW THE SOLAR SYSTEM

For many people, the terms "spaceflight" and "space exploration" immediately bring up images of humans walking on the moon and space probes traveling to the outer planets. Space missions have vastly expanded scientific

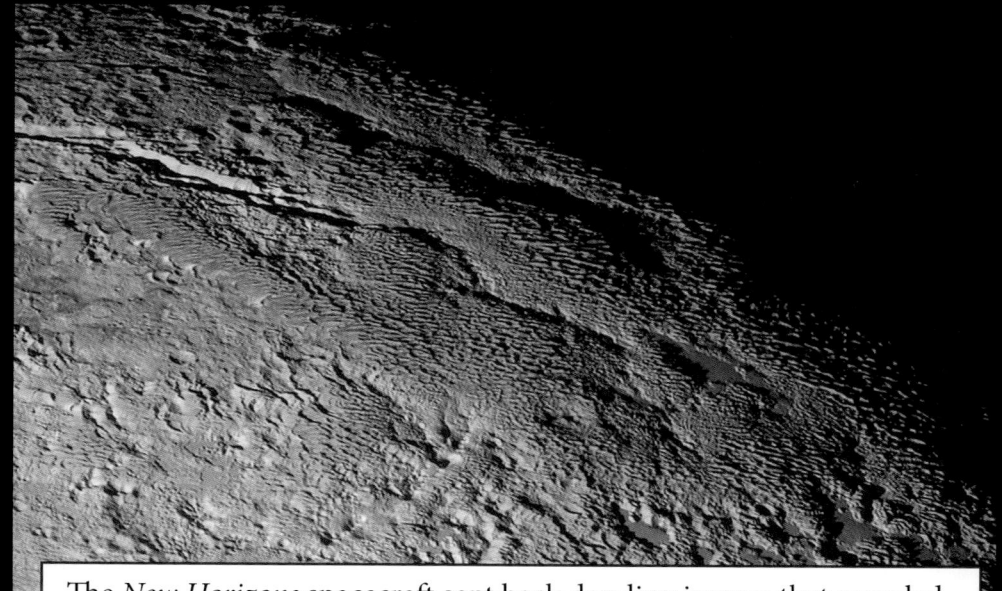

The *New Horizons* spacecraft sent back dazzling images that revealed surface features of Pluto that had never been seen before, such as bladelike ridges hundreds of feet tall.

Since landing on Mars in 2012, NASA's *Curiosity* rover has explored the planet's surface and analyzed samples with the objective of determining whether Mars could have ever supported life.

knowledge of the solar system. Ongoing projects, such as the *New Horizons* probe that passed by Pluto in 2015, and proposed exploration, such as a future manned expedition to Mars, continue to excite public interest.

Most space missions are launched with the objective of increasing human understanding of Earth's neighbors and conditions in outer space. This knowledge also helps scientists understand Earth and its interactions with other objects in the solar system. In addition, space is sometimes

THE COMET LANDER

In September 2016, the European Space Agency (ESA) probe *Rosetta* descended in a controlled landing on Comet 67P, ending a historic mission. Astronomers think that comets may contain some of the oldest and best-preserved material in the solar system—remnants of the building blocks that produced the planets Uranus and Neptune some 4.6 billion years ago. Comets remain essentially unchanged when they are away from the sun in the deep cold of space. Studying comets helps scientists understand how the solar system was formed.

Rosetta was the first spacecraft to orbit a comet. It circled Comet 67P for two years and deployed a lander to its surface. Unfortunately, the lander failed to anchor to the comet's surface and transmitted for less than three days. Nonetheless, the mission yielded significant new discoveries and data that will take years to analyze.

viewed as the last frontier, and people throughout history have always been lured to venture into the unknown.

Space research could potentially yield further tangible benefits in the future. For instance, detection systems are capable of identifying asteroids passing close to Earth, and technology of the future could potentially intercept an asteroid that would otherwise hit the planet. In addition,

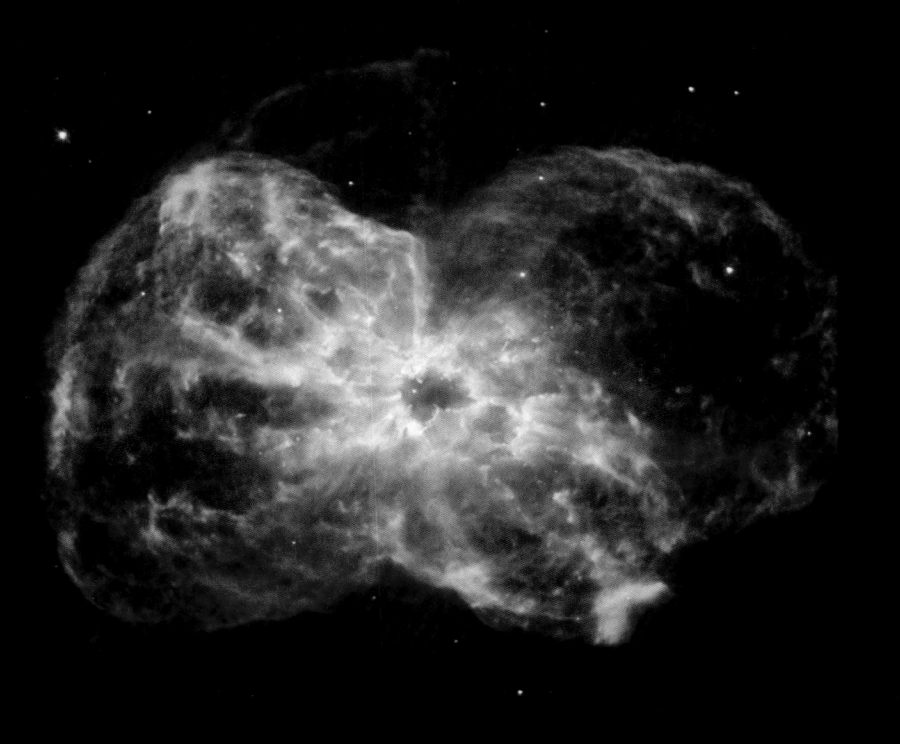

An image taken by the Hubble Space Telescope shows gas being emitted by a dying star—the ultimate fate of the sun in about five billion years.

advances in manned spaceflight could someday lead to a human colony on Mars.

EXPLORING OTHER BODIES

The solar system is a vast place, consisting of the sun, eight planets, nearly two hundred moons, several dwarf planets, hundreds of thousands of asteroids, and billions of comets. Most of what scientists know about the solar system comes from observation, using instruments on Earth or in space. Ground-based observatories collect and study visible light or radio waves emitted by objects in space. These are the two forms of radiation that reach the ground easily without being absorbed or scattered by Earth's atmosphere. Space-based observatories, such as the Hubble Space Telescope, have an advantage over ground-based instruments. They are able to detect types of radiation that are largely blocked by Earth's atmosphere—gamma rays, X-rays, ultraviolet radiation, and infrared radiation.

Unmanned space probes have also gathered data on many of the bodies in the solar system. These probes make flybys of bodies in space and sometimes orbit them, collecting images and taking measurements. Some probes land on the surface of a planet or other object to gather data. Space probes have explored all of the planets, Earth's moon, and many other celestial bodies. The two Voyager probes, launched in 1977, traveled past the outer planets of the solar system and continued flying outward. In 2013, *Voyager 1* reached interstellar space, about 12 billion miles (19 billion km) from the sun.

More space probes have been sent to Mars than any other planet. In addition to flyby missions and orbiters, NASA has landed mobile robotic rovers on Mars to explore the surface. Continued exploration by rovers could yield valuable data relevant for planning manned expeditions to Mars.

UNDERSTANDING EARTH'S EVOLUTION

As a result of research in the solar system, scientists have learned a great deal about the composition and geological features of Earth's neighbors. Some of the moons of the outer planets harbor vast oceans of water under icy crusts. Space has its own active weather system, mostly determined by solar activity. Some asteroids contain rare minerals that some people view as resources that could potentially be mined and exploited.

Studying the solar system has enabled scientists to better understand Earth's unique circumstances. Before the space age, scientists and visionaries speculated that intelligent life could exist on nearby planets. Observations and flybys revealed that Earth's nearest neighbors could not sustain life as it exists on Earth. Mars is too cold and dry, and temperatures on Venus are high enough to melt lead. Research from space missions has helped scientists to model the geological evolution of Venus, Earth, and Mars and learn why they turned out so different from one another.

In 2004, the *Cassini* spacecraft passed by and took pictures of Saturn. This composite image focuses on the planet's southern hemisphere, which is tipped toward the sun. Shadows cast by the rings are visible against the bluish northern hemisphere.

However, scientists have not given up hope that simple life-forms may exist on other planets or moons. Research on Earth and beyond has increased knowledge of climates and the conditions that make life possible. By studying how life initially formed on Earth, scientists can identify which other bodies in the solar system may be likely to harbor life and design new space missions to continue the search.

CHAPTER 5

EXPLORING GALACTIC FRONTIERS

The universe is so large that the vast Milky Way galaxy makes up only a tiny portion of it. Edwin Hubble showed in the 1920s that distant objects described as "nebulas" were actually neighboring galaxies. Today, it is known that billions of galaxies exist in the universe.

Some of the most exciting revelations about the universe outside the solar system and even beyond the Milky Way have been made by space telescopes. The best known is the Hubble Space Telescope, which has made discoveries that revolutionized astronomy. It has greatly expanded scientists' understanding of the big bang, the explosion from which the universe is thought to have originated. Hubble's successor, the James Webb Space Telescope, is scheduled to be launched in 2018.

THE LURE OF THE UNKNOWN

Studying outer space beyond the solar system is less likely to yield practical benefits than other applications of spaceflight technology, but it has the potential to enhance

Shown in an artist's depiction, the James Webb Space Telescope will have a mirror seven times larger than that of the Hubble Space Telescope and will orbit the sun.

scientific and even philosophical understanding of humankind's place in the universe. Discoveries based on distant observations can have direct relevance to physics and other fields of science as well.

Observations by space telescopes have helped provide clues to some of the basic questions about objects billions of miles away and events that happened billions of years in the past. Astronomers have been able to refine their estimates of the size of the universe and determine its age. Based partly on images from the Hubble Space Telescope, scientists have determined that the universe is about 13.75 billion years old.

Hubble and other space observatories have greatly increased knowledge of some of the most mysterious objects and phenomena in the universe. Scientists have been able

A picture from the Hubble Space Telescope shows a huge ring of gas and dust in space. Scientists think the ring may surround a black hole.

THE BIG BANG

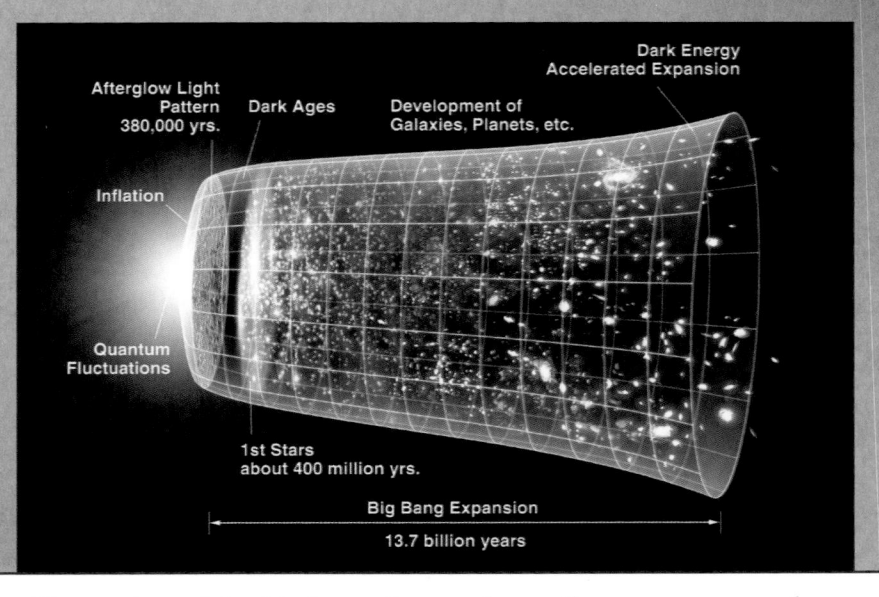

Dark Energy
Accelerated Expansion

Afterglow Light
Pattern
380,000 yrs.

Dark Ages

Development of
Galaxies, Planets, etc.

Inflation

Quantum
Fluctuations

1st Stars
about 400 million yrs.

Big Bang Expansion

13.7 billion years

An illustration of the big-bang theory shows the emergence and development of the universe beginning with the event known as inflation, a period of very fast expansion from a state of extremely high temperature and density.

The big-bang theory describes the emergence of the universe from a state of extremely high temperature and density. It's now known that the universe is still expanding, and observations with tools such as the Hubble Space Telescope help scientists calculate its rate of expansion. An aftereffect of the big bang is the cosmic microwave background radiation created by the explosion that now fills the universe. This background radiation can be measured with highly sensitive instruments that observe fluctuations in microwaves. Such research can help scientists understand what happened during the first few moments after the birth of the universe and forecast its ultimate destiny.

to study the physics of black holes, locate the source of gamma ray bursts, and map the distribution of dark matter. Researchers have observed regions undergoing star formation and caught images of supernovas—the violent explosions of giant stars.

SEARCHING FOR OTHER EARTHS

In 1995, scientists made the first discovery of an exoplanet orbiting a sunlike star. An exoplanet, or extrasolar planet, is a planet found outside the solar system. Astronomers had long believed that planets could form around other stars, but they had no means of detecting them. In the 1990s, scientists successfully identified the first few exoplanets. By the 2010s, new technology—especially the launch of space observatories specializing in hunting for exoplanets—had led to the discovery of thousands.

The first exoplanets found were gas giants that orbited close to their stars. As technology for identifying exoplanets was refined, scientists began identifying smaller planets as well. Some of these fell within their star's habitable zone—the distance at which life might take hold on the planet. In August 2016, astronomers discovered the nearest "Earth twin" yet orbiting Proxima Centauri, the star closest to the sun. This exoplanet, named Proxima b, was an exciting discovery because it was roughly the size of Earth and because it orbited within Proxima Centauri's habitable zone. Organic compounds, which make up life-forms, have been detected in the atmospheres of some exoplanets.

An artist's conception depicts Kepler-62f, an exoplanet about 1.4 times the size of Earth that orbits in the habitable zone of its star, which is seen peeking out from behind the right edge of the planet.

These discoveries have brought humankind a step closer to answering one of the fundamental questions that excites the imagination: are humans alone in the universe? Scientists are working on ways to recognize signs of life from afar. Future space observatories, such as the James Webb Space Telescope, will continue examining exoplanets. Such research could provide hints that there might be extraterrestrial life out there.

GLOSSARY

ASTEROID Any of the small rocky celestial bodies found especially between the orbits of Mars and Jupiter.

ASTRONOMER A scientist who studies stars, planets, and other objects in outer space.

ATMOSPHERE A shell of gases that surrounds a planet or star.

BLACK HOLE A celestial object that has a gravitational field so strong that light cannot escape it and that is believed to be created especially in the collapse of a very massive star.

CLIMATE The long-term pattern of weather in a particular place or region.

COMET A small celestial body orbiting the sun that appears as a fuzzy head usually surrounding a bright nucleus, that consists primarily of ice and dust, and that often develops one or more long tails when near the sun.

DEFIBRILLATOR A device that gives an electric shock to a person's heart to make it beat normally again, especially after a heart attack.

GALAXY Any one of the very large groups of stars that are found throughout the universe.

GEOLOGY A science that deals with the history of Earth and its life especially as recorded in rocks.

INVASIVE Involving entry into the body by cutting or by inserting an instrument.

METEOROLOGY A science that deals with the atmosphere and with weather.

MICROWAVE A comparatively short electromagnetic wave.

MISSION A flight by an aircraft or spacecraft to perform a specific task.

NAVIGATION The science of getting ships, aircraft, or spacecraft from place to place; the method of figuring out position, course, and distance traveled.

OBSERVATORY A building or place given over to or equipped for observation of natural phenomena (as in astronomy).

OCEANOGRAPHY A science that studies the oceans.

OPTICAL Of, relating to, or using light, especially instead of other forms of energy.

ORBIT A path followed by one body in its revolution about another.

POTABLE Safe to drink.

PROBE A device used to explore or send back information especially from outer space or a celestial body.

RADAR (**ra**dio **d**etecting **and r**anging) A device that sends out radio waves for finding out the position and speed of a moving object.

RECONNAISSANCE A survey to gain information.

SATELLITE A manufactured object or vehicle intended to orbit Earth, the moon, or another celestial body.

SOLAR PANEL A large, flat piece of equipment that uses the sun's light or heat to create electricity, or, a battery of solar cells (as in a spacecraft).

SOLAR SYSTEM The sun and the planets and other bodies that orbit around it.

SURVEY To measure and examine an area of land.

TRANSLUCENT Permitting the passage of light; clear.

TRANSMIT To send out a signal either by radio waves or over a wire.

FOR FURTHER READING

Bailey, Diane. *The Future of Space Exploration* (What's Next?). Mankato, MN: Creative Education, 2013.

DeYoe, Aaron. *Space Travel* (Out of this World). Minneapolis, MN: Super Sandcastle, 2016.

Mara, Wil. *Space Exploration* (Calling All Innovators). New York, NY: Children's Press, 2015.

Morgan, Ben, ed. *Space!* (Smithsonian Knowledge Encyclopedia). New York, NY: DK Publishing, 2015.

Paris, Stephanie. *21st Century: Mysteries of Deep Space* (Time for Kids Nonfiction Readers). Huntington Beach, CA: Teacher Created Materials, 2013.

Parks, Peggy J. *Space Research* (Inside Science). San Diego, CA: ReferencePoint Press, 2011.

Sparrow, Giles. *Space Exploration* (Space Travel Guides). Mankato, MN: Smart Apple Media, 2012.

Stott, Carole. *Space Exploration* (Eyewitness Books). New York, NY: DK Publishing, 2014.

Waxman, Laura Hamilton. *Exploring Space Travel* (Searchlight Books). Minneapolis, MN: Lerner Publications Company, 2012.

WEBSITES

Because of the changing nature of internet links, Rosen Publishing has developed an online list of websites related to the subject of this book. This site is updated regularly. Please use this link to access the list:

http://www.rosenlinks.com/FETTS/benefits

INDEX